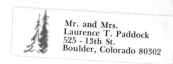

AMERICAN HORSE-DRAWN VEHICLES

AMERICAN HORSE-DRAWN VEHICLES

By JACK D. RITTENHOUSE

*Being a Collection of
Two Hundred and Eighteen Pictures
Showing
One Hundred and Eighty-Three
American Vehicles
(and Parts Thereof)
All Reproduced From
Fashion Plates of the Builders
or from
Little-Known Original Photographs*

BONANZA BOOKS · NEW YORK

NOTES ON USE OF THIS BOOK

The following notes are presented for the benefit of those readers who may wish to utilize illustrations in this book for purposes of research, model making, art source material or similar use.

REPRODUCTION. By use of a new chemical developer, the lithographer preparing this volume has been able to reproduce faithfully every line of the original. Any "broken lines" or other defects were in the original drawings, which have not been retouched, and are not the fault of the printer.

DATES. Where dates are shown, the date is that of the publication of the particular illustration shown, and indicates that the vehicle was used as early as that date. The date given is not that of the origin of the vehicle type shown. Most types had a European origin in their original form, and went through many decades of use before finally achieving popularity. To give proper dates of origin and duration would require extensive description beyond the province of this volume.

SCALE. The term, "scale: half-inch," means that a half-inch on the illustration is equal to one foot on the original vehicle.

TRACK. The term "track" refers to the extreme width of the vehicle as measured from the outside rim of one wheel to the outside of the rim of the opposite wheel, measured at the bottom of the wheel. Where more than one "track" dimension is given, the front track is always given first.

WHEELS. When wheel sizes are given, the dimensions refer to the height or diameter of the wheels, and where more than one wheel dimension is given, the height of the front wheels is given first.

SPOKES. Early drawings of carriage designs usually showed fewer spokes in the wheels than the wheels actually had. Where the phrase, "12 and 14 spokes," appears it indicates that the front wheels had 12 spokes and the rear wheels had 14 spokes. A few vehicles had all wheels alike.

BODY WIDTH. Extensive descriptions would be necessary to give all details of body widths on most carriages, since they had swelling sides, curving outward and upward from a relatively narrow floor. Unless specified as a seat width or other dimension, the width given is the floor width.

MODEL-MAKING. Given one dimension of a drawing, such as a wheel height, a competent modeler can determine other dimensions mathematically, if a scale is not given. Carriage makers, especially in England, often built models, which were usually on a scale of one or two inches to the foot.

COLORS. Color schemes given in descriptions were not mandatory on all vehicles of the type shown, but are simply colors used in a particular example. Most carriages were finished with paint and upholstery to suit the purchaser, formal vehicles in restrained colors; sporting vehicles permitted the use of brighter shades.

GEAR. The term "gear" is used herein to denote the general "undercarriage" parts comprising the wheels, axles, springs, pole, shafts, fifth-wheel, and related parts beneath the body itself.

SOURCES. The source of each illustration is given in a list at the end of the book. All dimensions, color schemes, and classifications are those of the source and not of the present compiler, and apply only to the example shown.

0-517-092573

© MCMXLVIII by Jack D. Rittenhouse

This edition published by Bonanza Books,
a division of Crown Publishers, Inc.,
by arrangement with Floyd Clymer Publications.

DEFGH

Manufactured in the United States of America

SOURCES OF ILLUSTRATIONS

Acknowledgment is made to the following sources for illustrations contained in this volume. Certain of the firms mentioned are no longer in business. References listed below give the page on which the illustration is found, with A or B indicating the top or bottom illustration, respectively, on the page listed.

ANHEUSER-BUSCH COMPANY, Saint Louis, Missouri. 93A.

APPLETON'S CYCLOPEDIA OF APPLIED MECHANICS. 8A, 98A, 99A-F.

JEROME BOLICK SONS COMPANY, Conover, North Carolina. 4B, 5A, 12A, 13A-B, 14A.

CHICAGO MUSEUM OF SCIENCE AND INDUSTRY, Chicago, Illinois. 40A-B, 41B, 88B, 98B.

COACH MAKERS' INTERNATIONAL JOURNAL. 9B, 10A, 11B, 17B, 23B, 28A-B, 30A-B, 32A, 33A, 34A, 35A, 49A, 52B, 53D, 73A-B, 75A, 84B.

EDISON INSTITUTE, Dearborn, Michigan. 72B.

G. S. ELLIS AND SON, Cincinnati, Ohio. 15A, 49B.

HUNTINGBURG WAGON WORKS, Huntingburg, Indiana. 3A-B, 12B.

JERALD SULKY COMPANY, Waterloo, Iowa. 50A-B, 51A-F.

KENTUCKY MANUFACTURING COMPANY, Louisville, Kentucky. 55A.

LANSING COMPANY, Lansing, Michigan. 67A-B.

J. B. LIPPINCOTT AND COMPANY, Philadelphia, Pennsylvania. 23A, 43A-B, 44A-B, 45A-B, 46A-B, 47A-B, 48B.

LOS ANGELES PUBLIC LIBRARY, Los Angeles, California. 16A, 20B, 35B, 37A, 16A, 89A.

METROPOLITAN MUSEUM OF ART, New York, N. Y. 4A, 8B.

J. D. MIRES AND SON, Earlville, New York. 74A.

OWENSBORO WAGON COMPANY, Owensboro, Kentucky. 18A, 54B, 55B, 56A-B, 58A-B, 59A-B, 60A-B, 61A-C, 62B, 63A-B, 64B, 65A-B, 66A-B, 68A-E, 69A-B, 70A-C, 71A-C, 82A, 85A, 86A-B, 87A-B, 90A-B, 91A, 92A, 93B, 94A-B, 95A-B, 96A-B, 97A-B.

RENICK, CURTIS AND COMPANY, Greencastle, Indiana. 11A.

FAIRMAN ROGERS, author of "Manual of Coaching." 23A, 43A-B, 44A-B, 45A-B, 46A-B, 47A-B, 48B.

THE STUDEBAKER CORPORATION, South Bend, Indiana. 9A, 38B, 39B, 41A, 57B.

SWAB WAGON COMPANY, Elizabethville, Pennsylvania. 54A, 62A, 67B, 75B, 77A-B, 78A-B, 79A, 81A, 83A, 84A.

THE HUB, periodical. 6A-B, 7A-B, 17A, 19B, 20A, 21B, 22B, 24B, 25A-B, 26A-B, 27A-B, 29A-B, 31A-B, 32B, 33B, 34B, 36A-B, 38A, 39A, 42A-B, 52A, 52A-C, 57A, 64A, 74B, 79B, 80A-B, 81B, 82B, 85B, 88A, 89B, 91B, 92B.

TITLE INSURANCE AND TRUST COMPANY, Los Angeles, California. 48A.

UNITED STATES NATIONAL MUSEUM, Washington, D. C. 37B.

WAYNESBURG CARRIAGE COMPANY, Waynesburg, O., 5B, 14B, 15B, 16B, 18B, 24A.

INTRODUCTION

HE PURPOSE of this book is to provide a collection of illustrations of prominent types of American horse-drawn vehicles. Such a collection has value for the artist, model-maker, teacher, and for the general public — which sees fewer and fewer of these vehicles as the years advance.

It would be impossible to present illustrations of every known type of American horse-drawn vehicle in a volume this size, or in one five times this size. This first volume is merely representative of several of the principal types of vehicles. Perhaps introduction of the subject through this initial book will induce others to extend the research and publication of more data on this aspect of American life.

The reader will notice a wide variation in names of apparently identical vehicles. Names were generic and applied to vehicles which were so classified on the basis of certain structural features, rather than on their entire detail. Minor variations in the design or location of seat, top, fenders, dashboard, springs, etc. (sometimes so minor as to be unnoticed at a quick glance) were often the only differences between styles offered by various carriage-makers. In addition, individual firms gave "trade names" to vehicles they designed, in an effort to gain distinction.

In studying or using the illustrations contained herein, the reader should keep the above information in mind. Where an illustration is captioned "victoria" or "landaulette," this is not to be construed as meaning that the vehicle shown is the absolute prototype, from which all others were copied, but it means merely that the example shown is generally typical of a victoria or a landaulette. The same qualification applies to a great many broad types of vehicles shown. However, each illustration has been prepared from a vehicle which was actually constructed.

For all practical considerations, the manufacture of carriages is a vanished craft. Vehicles used in harness racing, at horse shows and on farms are still being manufactured. However, the decline of the passenger carriage and commercial wagon began with the advent of the automobile at the turn of the century, and by the middle 1920's the carriage and wagon industry had become almost extinct.

Living persons and organizations rarely conceive themselves to be a part of history. As a consequence, they usually make no provision for the perpetuation of important data. When carriage plants closed their doors; when the more than forty carriage trade associations disbanded; when the technical schools for the craft ceased to exist, their literature was dispersed, destroyed and forgotten. Within another generation, original carriage literature will be extremely rare. It is already scarce. This condition was one of the impelling causes behind the preparation of this book.

In the compilation of illustrations for this book, efforts were made to secure clear drawings which revealed considerable detail. Many fine carriages still exist in America: in museums, on large estates, and stored in dusty barns and carriage houses. However, the usual photographs of these vehicles do not show construction details clearly, and in occasional instances the vehicles have been repaired or "restored" by workmen who altered basic details.

Although the horse-drawn vehicle is a vanishing object, it is by no means extinct. As long as there are horses and horse-lovers, there will be vehicles. It was estimated on January 1, 1947, that there were more than ten million horses on the farms of the United States. In 1890, there were eighteen million, and in 1920 there were twenty-six million horses. The typical farm wagon is still being built by many firms. Prices for gear (undercarriage and wheels) and a box body range from $100 to $250 for new wagons.

One carriage firm still in business in a small town in Indiana also continues to offer a limited line of new buggies, carts, surreys, etc., which they build to order in six weeks' time. Typical prices, quoted in late 1947, were about $75.00 for a two-wheeled phaeton cart, $135.00 or more for a buggy, and $215.00 or more for a surrey.

FORDER'S PATENT ROYAL HANSOM.
ALSO PATENTED IN THE UNITED STATES.

A New York firm, the Kauffman Saddlery Company, and a few others also deal in used carriages. Typical prices of vehicles are: victoria, $350.00; brougham, $350.00; cabriolet, $275.00; phaeton, $225.00; surrey, $275.00; break, $650.00; buggy, $125.00; and cart, $125.00. These are 1948 prices.

Before the turn of the century there were nearly 700 manufacturers who held membership in the Carriage Builders National Association. This number did not include many small firms or retailers. During this period, the Studebaker Company was credited with producing "a wagon every five minutes" of the working day, and an Indianapolis firm produced over 200,000 road carts in a single year. A company at Milwaukee, not a national leader, produced over 7,000 sleighs in a single season, and there were other instances of mass production reaching levels which are surprising to persons who believe only modern industry is capable of large output.

By 1890, the American carriage industry had reached its zenith, both in quantity and in quality. Well-to-do families maintained several vehicles. Fine carriages, such as broughams, sold for $1,000 to $2,000; victorias and landaus sold for $1,000 up. On the lower end of the scale, cheap buggies, wagons and sleighs sold for as low as $50.00. During this period, an average mechanic's wage was around $2.75 a day. The American carriage industry taught the world how to build lightweight but rugged carriages and shipped its vehicles to all countries.

The carriages remaining from this "hay-day" are rapidly disappearing. Anyone possessing a carriage "handed down" from previous generations would perform a genuine public service were they to offer the vehicle to a museum when they no longer have an interest in keeping it. Any public library can provide a list of museums.

To a similar degree, old carriage makers' catalogs, plans, magazines, wall charts, scrapbooks, technical books and similar literature should be placed in the hands of responsible persons. Even tattered copies are of value to the researcher, librarian and curator. Each year, the sum of such material remaining in the nation is reduced.

AMISH BUGGY. (Scale: about half-inch.) The Amish sect of Indiana, Ohio and Pennsylvania are forbidden by their creed to use autos. Their buggies (shown here without top) are still built by a few small firms.

AUTO-SEAT TOP BUGGY. The buggy was a truly distinctive American type of vehicle, popular because of its lightness and economy. The seat style shown here was similar to that used on early autos.

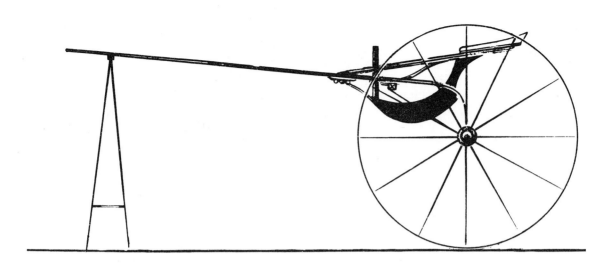

JOGGING CART. A very light two-wheeler, generally with a slat bottom. It carried one or two passengers and was used for light country work and for exercising trotters, "jogging" them around. Similar vehicles of modern design are shown on later pages of this volume, devoted to harness racing carts.

CUT-UNDER BUGGY. The arched construction of the body beneath the seat gave clearance to the wheels when making sharp turns. It also gave more "style." Elliptic springs, shown at front and rear, were invented in 1804.

PONY SURREY. A small, light surrey to be drawn by one or two ponies. Body was 30 inches wide, with wheels 30 and 38 inches. (Smaller wheel size given in all descriptions is always for front wheel.) Track, or width from outside of one wheel to outside of opposite wheel, was 45 inches.

Detailed view of patent spring used on road wagon shown below.

SLAT-BOTTOM ROAD WAGON. Extremely light and springy, this wagon was often used as a businessman's vehicle. Arched slats made a resilient floor, and there was ample baggage space in back. Body was 26 inches wide.

WHITECHAPEL BUGGY WITH STICK SEAT. (Period: 1885; scale: one-half inch.) The seat style was so named because of the "sticks" used in its sides. Note arrangement of side bar springs on this vehicle. Body was 30 inches wide on top, 27 inches wide on bottom. Track: 52 inches. Gear painted blue.

BUSINESS BUGGY. (Scale: half-inch.) Rattan sides gave this buggy an elegant style. Body 28 inches wide; track 56 inches. So named because of the roomy section in the rear of the body, useful for sample cases and parcels.

BUCKBOARD WITH RUMBLE. (Period: 1890; scale: half-inch.) The original buckboard had a seat mounted on a single board bolted to front and rear axles, with no springs. Later several slats replaced the single board, but this model used one oak board 29 by 87 inches. Wheels 40 and 45 inches; 12 and 14 spokes; track 56 inches. The term "rumble seat" began with carriages.

DOCTOR'S WAGON. (Period: 1890; scale: half-inch.) The use of canework on bodies was popular in the 1890's. Body of this model was black, with green trim and silver mountings. Wheels 36 and 48 inches; 12 and 14 spokes; track 56 inches. Doctors' vehicles usually had large folding tops.

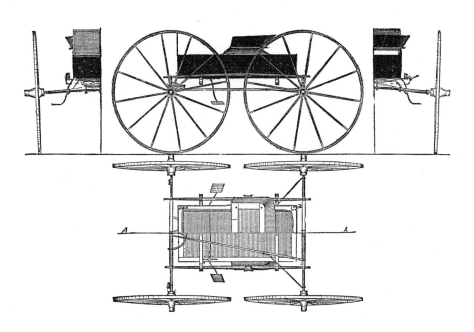

BUGGY CONSTRUCTION. Four views from an encyclopedia of 1880, showing profile (center), half of front end (left), half of rear end (right), and a composite view (bottom) showing view from above (section above line A-A) and view from below (beneath line A-A). Wheels shown were four feet high.

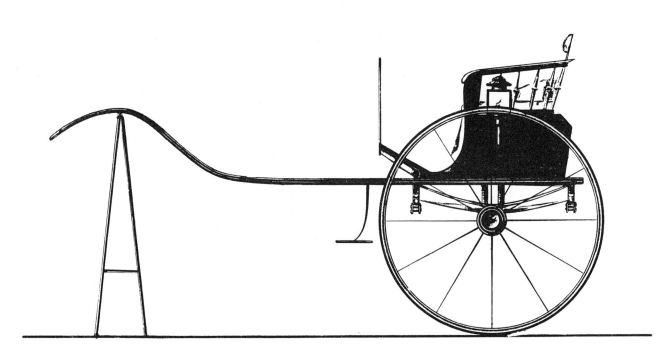

STANHOPE GIG. Used extensively in England and in the Eastern parts of the United States. It is still in occasional use for showing one or a tandem of hackneys or hackney ponies at horse shows. Example shown was a design by the famous Brewster company. Note lamps. (Scale: about half-inch.)

BIKE WAGON. A light driving wagon with "bike" axles. Body was 22 by 56 inches, with padded leather dash, velvet carpet and blue upholstery. Body black; gear (undercarriage) carmine. Track 36 inches wide.

COAL BOX BUGGY. (Scale: half-inch.) The name was a term of derision, since the body resembled a grocer's coal box. Body was 30 inches wide; wheels 48 and 50 inches; track 58 inches. Painted lake red with gold stripes.

DONKEY CART. (Scale: about half-inch.) An English design, sometimes known as a "tub" or "pony cart," and often used by children. Two seats, placed lengthwise, with an "underslung" axle. For a similar vehicle, see the governess cart shown on page 21 of this volume.

JUMP-SEAT WAGON. (Scale: half-inch.) The front seat of this wagon folded down and back, while the rear seat "jumped" forward to make the vehicle a single-seater. This light wagon was frequently equipped with side curtains. Body was 40 inches wide; wheels 46 and 49 inches.

ROAD CART. (Period: 1884; scale unknown.) A light vehicle on extra long elliptic springs (shown at left in detail). Note the unique bend of the long shafts. This type was an unusually well balanced pleasure cart.

JENNY LIND. (Scale: half-inch.) A "Jenny Lind" was an early type of buggy with a fixed top. Named for the famous singer. Usually of elaborate design and painting. Body 30 inches wide; wheels 47 and 50 inches.

STICK-SEAT SLAT WAGON. Lightness and elegance combined in this wagon, with a slat floor on front-to-back "Concord" springs. Ornamental iron braces and an upswept front end added grace. Padded leather dashboard.

SPRING WAGON. This wagon is still built in one or two American shops. It might be called "the poor man's surrey," because it is essentially a family vehicle, although its rear seat could be removed when necessary.

LIGHT PONY WAGON. This small, colorful vehicle had a black body with gear painted wine, yellow or carmine. Green upholstery. This body style was known as a "piano box." Body 19 by 45 inches; wheels 32 and 34 inches; 45-inch track. Shafts used on this wagon were 54 inches long.

CUT-UNDER RUNABOUT. City driving required sharp turns into driveways and alleys, and this necessitated the "cut-under" construction which gave clearance to the front wheels when turning in a small radius. In the 1890's, rubber tires, either solid or semi-pneumatic, were often used.

PARASOL-TOP PONY RUNABOUT. The parasol-type top was often used on many town carriages. Upholstery here was green; body black; gear wine or yellow. Steel wheels 32 and 34 inches; 45-inch track. Body 19 inches wide.

PHAETON. The phaeton was a four-wheeled carriage with open sides. It was named for the Greek god who drove the chariot of the sun. The type of phaeton shown here was often used by ladies, sometimes by businessmen.

HIGH TANDEM GIG. A sporting vehicle with a dashing appearance. Competent drivers usually considered them unsafe, however, because of their height. Shown here with a single horse. (Note fly net.) When used with a tandem hitch, a pair of horses were used "in line," or head to tail.

SIDE-SEATED PLATFORM WAGON. Used by hotels and resorts to convey guests from railroad "depots." Also frequently used at funerals. Body was 9 by 3 feet, with three springs at front and rear. It was equipped with fringed top, brake and removable seats. Body was wine color, gear yellow.

GAME CART. A light, sporting vehicle which could be used with four horses. Vehicles of this type are still seen on large, fashionable estates. It was the only type of four-wheeler which custom permitted to be used for a tandem.

FRINGED TOP SURREY. Famed in song and story is this capacious family vehicle with its sweeping fenders and leather dash. Furnished with oil lamps, velvet carpet and blue cloth upholstery. Wheels 40 and 44 inches, with 56-inch track. Body was usually black, with gear in Brewster green.

BUCKBOARD. (Scale: half-inch.) The example shown was a variation of the buckboard type, with intricate front bracing designed to reduce jars and rattling. The buckboard was considered far more comfortable in rough country and for long trips than its simple design would ordinarily suggest.

BASKET PHAETON. (Scale: half-inch.) A light vehicle for two. The design shown is from an 1870 magazine. Basket phaetons frequently had a single rumble seat. They did not have the heavy appearance of phaetons with painted wood panels. Wheels 33 and 42 inches; track 58 inches; seat 36 inches wide.

LADIES' STANHOPE. (Scale: about half-inch.) An elegant light vehicle, more stylish than a buggy, graceful and easy to manage on city streets.

AUTO-TOP SURREY. Not all surreys had fringed tops, as this example proves. Top on this model folded back in fair weather. Upholstery was of whipcord or broadcloth. Example shown had wheels 40 and 44 inches high. Body was painted in black and carmine, with gear in green and gold.

THREE-SEAT PLATFORM WAGON. A vehicle used chiefly in rural districts, where it was often "hired out" by livery stables. It had a canopy top and a body nine feet long by three feet wide. Also made 10½ feet long, with four seats. Body was black with carmine wheels. "Platform" springs in front.

ROCKAWAY OR DEPOT WAGON. (Scale: half-inch.) The name of this wagon indicates its customary use. Body was 36 inches wide on floor; wider across top. Furnished with rolled curtains, green leather upholstery and silver mountings. Wheels 40 and 48 inches; track five feet.

LIGHT DROP-FRONT PHAETON. (Period: 1885; scale: half-inch.) Phaetons varied widely in style and in top design. Canopy, umbrella or bow tops were used. Width of this body was 41 inches at center. Wheels 36 and 44 inches; with 53-inch track. Body was painted blue, with brass mountings.

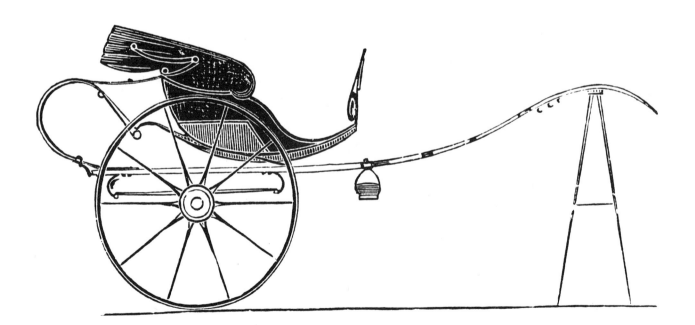

CABRIOLET. (Period: about 1840.) A two-wheeled vehicle poised on the "C-springs" used in early days. When turned out by the quality, a small-sized groom called a "tiger" stood on the rear platform and held on to tasseled straps.

GOVERNESS CART. Used for governess and several children, and was also used by children for driving ponies. Slightly larger than a "pony cart," the governess cart usually had sides, back and front made of basket work which flared out at the top. Wheels 30 or 36 inches high, track 43 inches.

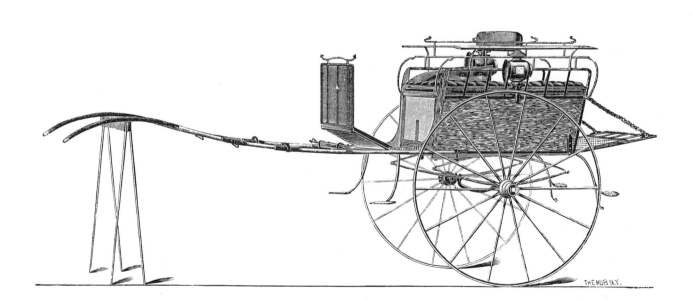

DOG CART. (Period: 1890; scale: half-inch.) The dog cart was originally used to transport hunting dogs, but later became a fashionable cart for general use. Passengers rode back to back. Ample storage space beneath seats. Body 38½ inches wide; wheels 50 inches; 14 spokes; 59-inch track.

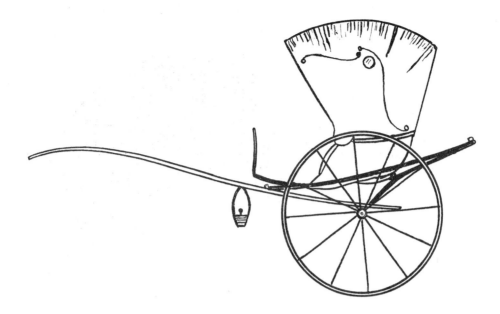

ONE-HORSE "SHAY" (CHAISE). Made famous by the poem about the wonderful "one-hoss shay" that ran a hundred years. A chaise was a two-wheeled vehicle with a folding top and with a body suspended on unique "springs" extending from upturned rear ends of shafts to a point forward of the wheels.

BRUNSWICK. (Period: 1890; scale: about three-eighths-inch.) The Brunswick was a type of vehicle related to the surrey: a two-seated, four-wheeled carriage, but it had a fixed top. Note elliptic springs at front and rear. These are the type of springs shown herein on vehicles of the 1865-1870 period, although the drawings do not always show them clearly.

PRIVATE OMNIBUS. (Period: 1895; scale unknown.) A vehicle drawn by four horses or three horses abreast. Used in some sections as a station wagon. Passengers entered from the rear, and this allowed the use of large, easy-riding wheels in back. Grooms' seats could be attached to rear.

CANOPY-TOP WAGONETTE. (Scale: half-inch.) A fashionable eight-passenger vehicle used at "watering places." Passengers entered from the rear and sat face to face. Top could be removed or "shifted." Curved line above the rear wheel indicated a fender. Body was brown with black gear.

TRAP. A vehicle with an unusual body arrangement: front seat divided to allow access to rear seat; back of rear seat could fold down forward when not in use. Sometimes equipped with canopy top. Body 33 inches wide; wheels 41 and 45 inches, with 56 inch track. Flat, wooden arm-rest "fenders." Body was black; gear green; upholstery of blue broadcloth or corduroy.

FOUR-PASSENGER STANDING-TOP PHAETON. (Period: 1886; scale: half-inch.) Light vehicles of this type were made in many parts of America, designated by various local names. Note doors, side curtains and rear spring arrangement. Body 35 inches wide. Wheels 40 and 47 inches, 56-inch track.

ESSEX TRAP. (Period: 1893; scale: half-inch.) Shown as arranged when passengers rode back to back. Could be arranged so all seats faced forward. As in all traps, passengers could enter rear seat through front. Body was 35 inches wide. Wheels 42 and 48 inches high, with 56-inch track.

SIX-PASSENGER CANOPY-TOP PHAETON. (Period: 1890; scale, half-inch.) This vehicle had two seats in the rear compartment, facing each other. Top was removable. Body was 35 inches wide on floor, with seats 42 inches wide. Length of body: 99 inches. Wheels 34 and 42 inches; 10 and 12 spokes; 54-inch track. Total weight: 700 lbs. Body and gear were green

LADIES' DRIVING PHAETON. (Period: 1890; scale: half-inch.) This elegant vehicle appeared best when drawn by two horses. The "skeleton rumble" seat in the rear was for the footman. The intricate and graceful frame of this vehicle was typical of the "golden age" of carriage making.

LADIES' DRIVING PHAETON. (Scale: half-inch.) Note the rattan-work sides of the seats, the sweeping dash and the parasol top of this vehicle. Body was 36 inches wide on the floor, 44½ inches wide at top. Wheels 27 and 35 inches, 12 and 14 spokes with track of 39 inches in front and 55 inches at rear.

SPIDER PHAETON. (Period: 1885; scale: half-inch.) A fashionable driving vehicle for gentlemen, with "skeleton rumble" seat for footman. Notice the intricately curved iron "body loops" or frame from front to rear. Body 46 inches wide at seat. Wheels 34 and 44 inches; 51-inch track.

STANHOPE PHAETON. (Period: 1887; scale: half-inch.) A vehicle usually used by two persons but having seats for two more in back. The sides of this model were cut down more than was usual. Note rattan panels. Body 29 inches wide on floor. Wheels 32 and 41 inches; 55-inch track.

FULL CLARENCE. (Period: 1865; scale: three-eighths-inch.) The clarence had a single upholstered seat across the back, with a curved glass front. Below the curved glass, inside the body, was a hinged seat for two more adults. This example shows the retention of the C-spring at the rear.

TWELVE-QUARTER COACH. (Period: 1869; scale: half-inch.) This coach had 12 quarters, or panels: three on each side, three at front and rear. Panels could all be removed in summer, or a few removed in spring or fall, thus allowing more "air" as the seasons changed. Body 53 inches wide. Wheels 44 and 50 inches, 60-inch track. Body and gear plum color.

COUPE. (Period: 1854; scale unknown.) The coupe derived its name from the French word meaning "cut," since it resembled a coach which had been cut in half. The design shown closely resembled a sedan-brougham.

COUPE. (Period: 1868; scale: half-inch.) American coupes usually had a curved front glass and a hinged child's-seat inside, below the glass. (See brougham.) One wide seat for adults. Body of this example was 52 inches wide. Wheels 40 and 46 inches; track 58 inches. Satin upholstery.

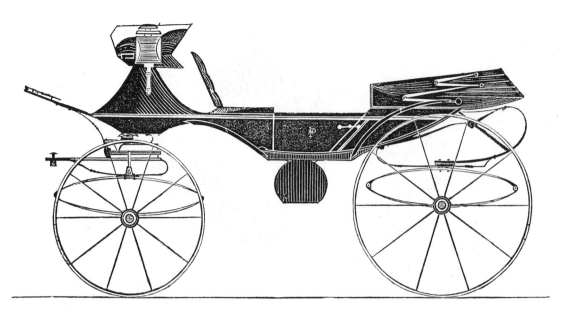

BRETT. (Scale: half-inch.) The fashionable brett was a vehicle with a shallow body, with a bow-top over the rear, and with a front seat facing to the rear and having a hinged back. Body shown was 48 inches wide. Wheels 40 and 48 inches; track 5 feet. Body purple, gear black. Morocco trim.

ROUND BOTTOM BRETT. (Scale: half-inch.) The brett was a modified and somewhat lighter-weight vehicle than the barouche or caleche. This example had a purple body with plum colored gear. Brown cloth upholstery. Mountings: gold.

VICTORIA. (Scale: half-inch.) One of the most gracious of all carriages, said to have been named for Queen Victoria. Width of seat 47½ inches; floor 31 inches wide at toe-board; wheels 30 and 41 inches; wheels had 10 and 12 spokes; track was 44 and 54 inches.

BROUGHAM. (Scale: half-inch.) Introduced in England in 1837; named for Lord Brougham. There were depot broughams, country broughams, bachelors' broughams, miniature broughams, etc. Body shown above was 40 inches wide. Wheels 35 and 47 inches; 10 and 12 spokes; track 48 and 56 inches.

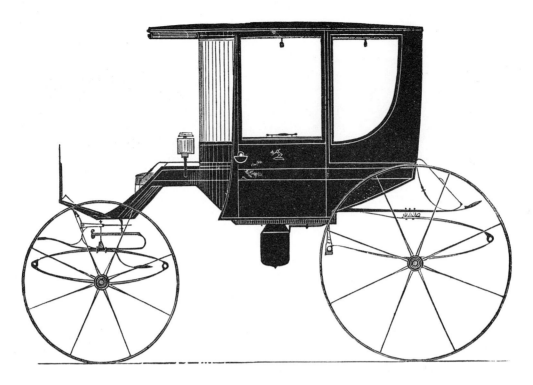

CLARENCE ROCKAWAY. (Period: 1870; scale: half-inch.) A rockaway had a driver's seat built into the body and had a top projecting over the driver's seat. It was difficult to design a handsome rockaway. Body 50 inches wide; wheels 41 and 49 inches; track 5 feet. Body green; gear carmine.

CURTAIN-QUARTER ROCKAWAY. (Period: 1885; scale: half-inch.) Rockaways usually had the rear quarters (panels) designed for both glass and curtains, interchangeable seasonally. Body 47½ inches wide; wheels 37 and 48 inches; 12 and 14 spokes; track 56 inches. Color: all green.

LANDAULETTE. (Period: 1868; scale: half-inch.) The landau was first designed in Landau, Germany, and had folding tops at front and rear. Usually the landaulette had such a top only at the rear. Solid front was removable. Body 51 inches wide; wheels 44 and 48 inches; track 5 feet.

ROUND-FRONT LANDAULETTE. (Period: 1884; scale: half-inch.) This ancestor of the modern "convertible" had a round front which was lowered in fine weather. Note "pump handle" arms extending to rear atop springs. Body was 50 inches wide; wheels 36 and 47 inches; track 48 and 56 inches.

PEABODY VICTORIA. (Period: 1865; scale: half-inch.) Compare this earlier victoria with the one shown on page 31 to note basic lines of the type. The elliptical spring open at front was typical of the period. Body was 47 inches wide at seat; wheels 40 and 46 inches high, front and rear respectively.

EIGHT-SPRING CALECHE. (Scale: half-inch.) Resembling a barouche, the caleche was a French importation: an open carriage with long, sweeping lines. Note the intricate springing, with straps to prevent excessive swaying of the body when in motion.

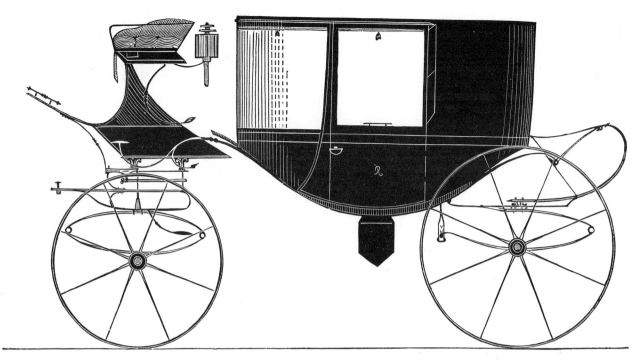

CHARIOT. (Scale: half-inch.) The chariot was the last of the colonial coach types, and was the forerunner of the brougham and coupe. Bodies were colorful: this example had claret panels and a belt of sea green. Undercarriage was emerald. Trimmed in green satin. Ivory mountings.

POST CHAISE. (Scale: half-inch.) Fitted with leather cases for traveling. Notice the bar extending from front axle to rear to give strength. C-springs were the only ones used at the time. Seats were provided at front and rear for coachman and footmen.

PONY BREAK. (Period: 1890; scale: half-inch.) The "break" was originally designed for use in "breaking" or training coach horses but soon became a light sporting vehicle to be drawn by four horses or ponies. Body was 35½ inches wide. Track 56 inches. Weight of this model was 550 lbs.

GENTLEMEN'S DRIVING PHAETON. (Period: 1890; scale: half-inch.) That this was a masculine vehicle is evident from the absence of intricate curves. The side panels were not basketry, but resembled silver or bronze. Body was 31 inches wide on floor; wheels 36 and 48 inches; track 55 inches.

SIGHTSEEING WAGON. (Period: 1875.) This weird "contraption" was designed to accommodate a surprising number of people, but its rococo lines were too extreme to make the style acceptable for long.

COACHEE. This example, shown in the U. S. National Museum, had C-springs made of hickory. Passengers entered from the rear. In Philadelphia, in 1794, 847 pleasure carriages were taxed, including "33 coaches, 157 coachees, 35 chariots, 22 phaetons, 80 light wagons, and 520 chairs and sulkies."

LANDAU. (Scale: about three-eighths inch.) Some had glass sides. In contrast to the landaulette, the landau usually had folding bow tops at both ends. Top here was all leather. Morocco upholstery. Body was 55 inches wide in center; track 54 inches in front and 61 inches in rear.

PRESIDENT GRANT'S LANDAU. (Period: about 1875.) The Studebaker Company built this landau especially for President Grant. It shows the front top folded forward, behind the driver's seat. Six-horse teams were not uncommon on these large, heavy vehicles. (Studebaker photo.)

PANEL-BOOT VICTORIA. (Scale: half-inch.) A feature here was the folding seat behind the driver's seat, used by a child. The victoria was fashionable as a park vehicle. Body 48½ inches wide at seat; wheels 34 and 44 inches; 12 and 14 spokes; track 48 and 56 inches.

PANEL-BOOT VICTORIA. The terms "cabriolet" and "victoria" were apparently used loosely by carriage makers, for varying names were given for almost identical vehicles. The few photographs in this volume have been included to show proportions not indicated by drawings. Each type of vehicle had its own style of harness. (Studebaker photo.)

LAFAYETTE'S CARRIAGE. (Period: 1824.) When LaFayette revisited America, long after the Revolutionary War, he was wildly acclaimed, showered with gifts, feted by Jefferson, Monroe and Adams. The American people presented him with this carriage, known later as the caleche type. The intricate springs merit attention. Footman stood on rear platform.

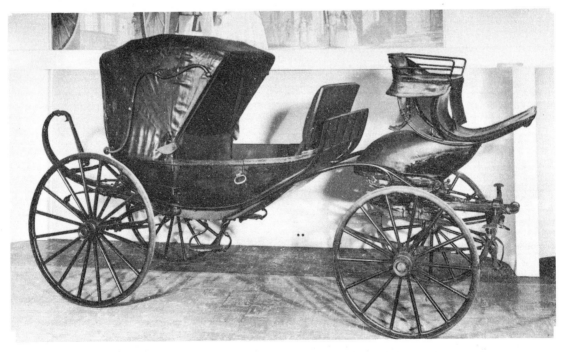

LINCOLN'S CARRIAGE. Abraham and Mary Todd Lincoln are reported to have ridden in this carriage the afternoon of the day of his assassination. Its style was that of a caleche or barouche (two names for the same type of carriage). The structure beneath the seat was called a "boot."

SURREY. This photograph of a canopy-top surrey reveals the smartness of this popular "turn-out," although it indicates at the same time how the usual photograph obscures details of construction. Such details are shown best only in carriage makers' illustrations. (Studebaker photo.)

McKINLEY'S CARRIAGE. (Period: 1900.) This is an example of a panel-boot victoria, sometimes incorrectly called a "cabriolet." It shows the appearance of the vehicle with the top raised, most illustrations showing the top down. The pole has been slung beneath the carriage. (Museum of Science & Industry.)

MYLORD. (Scale: half-inch.) This is actually a panel-boot victoria, but the American manufacturer catalogued it with the swank name (frequently used in France) in the hope of attracting prospective buyers. The example shown was displayed at the Columbian Exposition in Chicago, in 1893.

OCTAGON-FRONT COUPE. (Period: 1890; scale: half-inch.) Three frames were often used in place of expensive curved glass for carriage fronts. Body was dark blue and black, upholstered in blue goatskin and blue satin. Body 8½ feet long, 51 inches wide. Wheels 35 and 44 inches.

BREAK. (Period: 1895; scale unknown.) Compare this "break" with the one shown on page 36. This is an example of the true "break," a vehicle used in "breaking" horses. The shaft extending from front axle to rear was known as a "perch." Note absence of rear springs on this example.

0 1 2 3 4 5 6 7 8 9 10

CHAR-A-BANCS BREAK. (Period: about 1885; scale: half-inch.) The name was derived from the French, meaning a car with benches placed across it. The example shown weighed about 1600 lbs., being lighter than a coach.

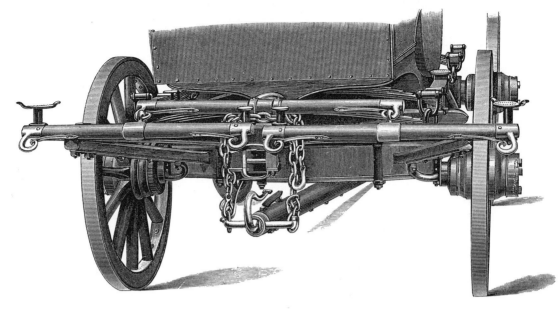

VIEW OF FRONT OF ROAD COACH. (Period: 1895.) A detailed view of the front gear of a road coach similar to the coach shown below. Tongue has been slung beneath axles. This was done when the vehicle was stored or when it was parked at races, while passengers viewed the meet.

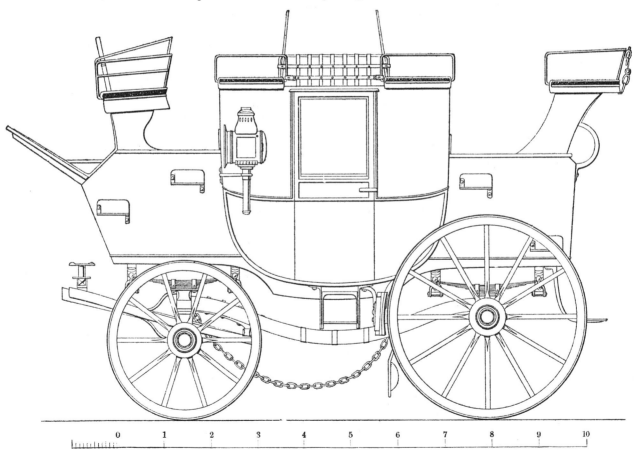

ROAD-COACH. (Period: 1898; scale: half-inch.) As previously mentioned, the road-coach was chiefly a commercial vehicle, although a few were used for private driving. This example was built by the firm of Brewster & Company, noted as America's most distinguished stylists of fine carriages.

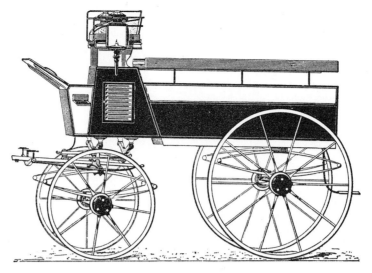

WAGONETTE. (Period: 1890; scale unknown.) Compare the wagonette shown here with the "break" shown on page 43. Note the absence here of the perch, and the use of rear springs. This made the vehicle easier on the team, since it absorbed much of the shock otherwise felt by the horses. Passengers entered from the rear and sat on seats which ran along the sides.

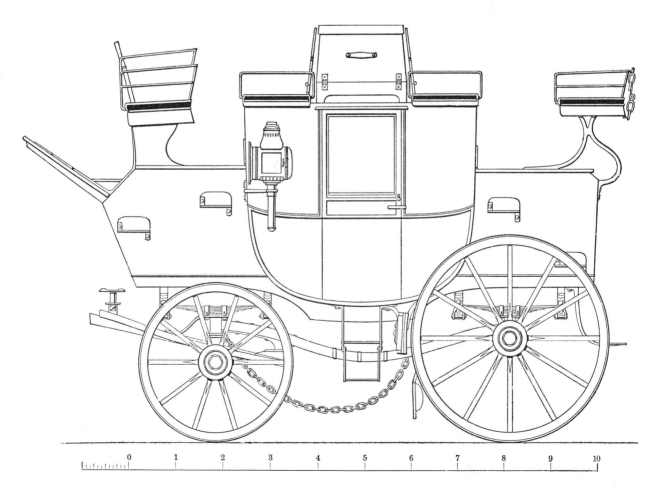

DRAG. (Period: 1895; scale: half-inch.) Another example of the carriages built by the famous Brewster firm. The "drag" was used only for private coaching, but it greatly resembled the "road-coach" shown on the previous page. Several drags still survive, used by sportsmen and by resorts.

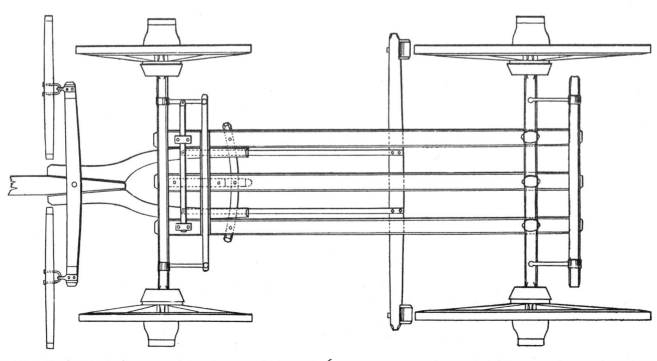

HEAVY CONCORD COACH. (Period: 1890; scale: half-inch.) Profile view
shown above and view of undercarriage shown below.
Further views on next page.

CONCORD COACH. The name of this famous coach came from its place of origin: Concord, New Hampshire. The best ones were built by the famous firm of Abbot-Downing Company, whose drawings are shown on these two pages. Heavy coaches were used in the West and shipped to South Africa. Lighter models were used in the Eastern States.

In structure, it resembled the English coach of the 18th century. In function, it served perfectly on the rough roads of the early West. The ample body, almost egg-shaped in its tri-dimensional curves, was a fine piece of joinery. It rested upon two lengthwise "thorough-braces," each of several leather strips. These helped absorb shocks which would otherwise affect the 6-horse team. The thorough-braces were attached to stiff iron standards.

Concord coaches weighed 2,500 lbs., and sold for $1,250 or more. They carried nine passengers inside and as many more as could cling to the roof.

Shown on this page are a rear view and a contemporary photograph, both views by the Abbot-Downing Company.

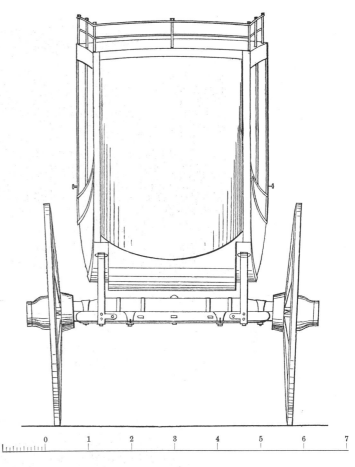

0   1   2   3   4   5   6   7

MUD-WAGON. (Period: about 1880.) The "mud-wagon" was a type of stage-coach which might be called "the poor man's Concord." While it used thorough-braces, their method of attachment was simpler. One difference was in the body, with its flat sides and simpler joinery. Note the three-horse lead team.

LIGHT CONCORD COACH. (Period: about 1880.) This is an example of the lighter model of the Concord coach, built for use on Eastern roads where conditions were not so rugged as in the West. It was somewhat smaller in nearly all respects. (Photo by Abbot-Downing Company, Concord, N.H.)

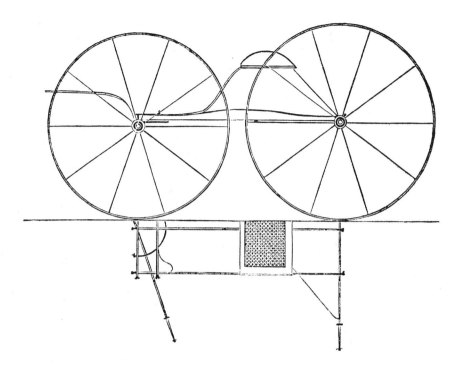

SKELETON WAGON. (Scale: half-inch.) An extremely light, one-man, racing vehicle with spokes not much thicker than a lead pencil. Seat was 13 by 20 inches, with silver rail on each side. Wheels 47 and 49 inches; 52-inch track.

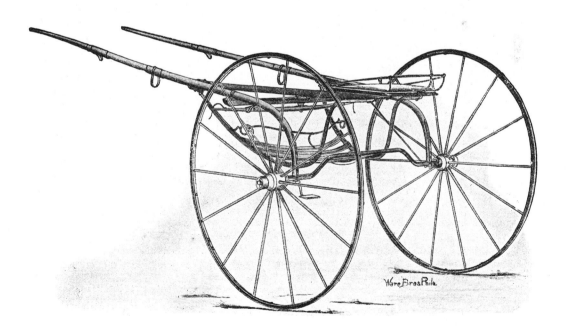

ROAD CART. (Period: 1910.) A light, fast cart used in exercising harness racing horses. From 1870 on, carts like this were often used for racing. Wheels 4 feet high; steel tires; weight 100 to 125 lbs. Painted in red and green.

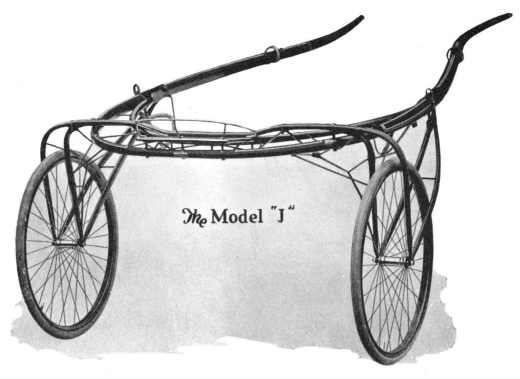

HARNESS RACING SULKY. View of a modern vehicle currently manufactured. Height, under arch: 27 inches; shafts: 87 inches from tip to arch. Wheels 26 or 28 inches high, with 53-inch track. Color green with gold stripes.

FINE HARNESS BUGGY. Another vehicle still being manufactured and often used in horse shows. Body 16 by 52 inches; wheels 26 inches high; 48-inch track. Chrome wheels, patent leather dash, maroon cushion and rug. Body maroon with vermillion stripes. Further views on next page.

HARNESS RACING SULKY. Closeup view showing details of construction. Metal cane seat.

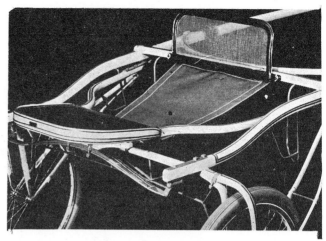

HARNESS RACE CART. Used for long-gaited horses. 41 inch track. Safer than most racing sulkies.

JOGGING AND EXERCISE CART. Solid rubber tires. Wheels 40 inches; track 53 inches; shafts 88 inches.

COMBINATION CART. Used for exercise and training of harness racing horses. Similar to cart above.

HARNESS BUGGY. A light show-buggy in maroon color. Body 17 by 52 inches; wheels 28 inches high.

HARNESS BUGGY. Modern, like all shown on this page. A one-man, one-horse, show vehicle.

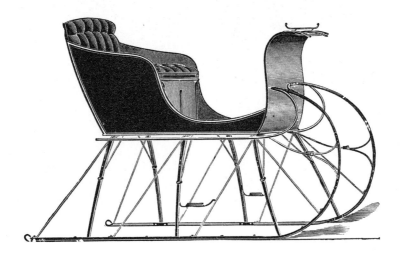

BUFFALO SPEEDING CUTTER. (Period: 1887; scale: five-eighths-inch.) A typical light sleigh of which many examples remain. Body was black, lined with gold; running part was vermillion. Seat 31 inches wide; gear 22 inches high; track 42 inches; body 25 inches wide beneath floor. Gold mountings.

ONTARIO 6-PASSENGER SLEIGH. (Period: 1870; scale: half-inch.) There were many types of sleighs other than the traditional one seen so often. The body of this example had rounded, swelling sides, with a swan's head at the front. Track 42 inches. Finished emerald green; green plush cushions.

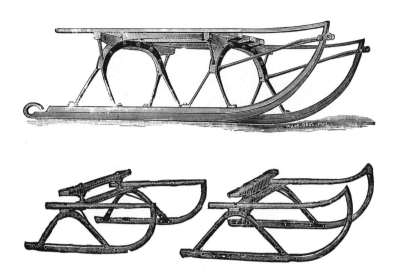

BOB SLEIGHS. (Period: 1895; scale unknown.) In winter, any farm or commercial vehicle could be converted into a bobsled by simply attaching the body to "bobs" such as these. Usually made of select bent wood, the bobs also could be made in heavier styles than the examples shown above.

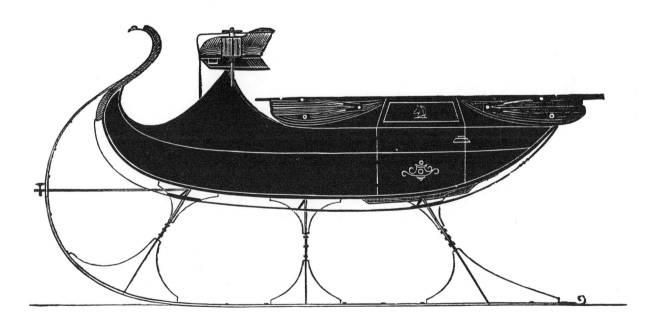

LANDAU SLEIGH. (Period: 1869; scale: half-inch.) The finest sleighs had bodies built along the same lines as carriages. Shown here is a landau body on runners. Example shown was the first in America, and few were made. A heavy vehicle, it had a body 50 inches wide. Folding tops; lamps; morocco leather upholstery. Body was colored purple lake; running gear carmine.

SPRING WAGON. A handy, one-horse wagon equipped with elliptical springs, wooden dasher and brake. Body 90 by 40 inches; wheels 38 and 42 inches; weight 600 lbs.; load capacity 800 lbs. Body and gear wine color.
(Note: where no period is indicated on following pages, vehicle was built and used as late as 1920. Scale given only where accurate data was available.)

SPRING-WAGON WITH CUT-UNDER WHEELS. Small front wheels on this wagon could turn beneath the bed. This wagon sold for about $80.00 and could haul 900 lbs. Wheels 34 and 46 inches; body 84 by 40 inches.

ONE-HORSE FARM WAGON. A light, standard utility wagon. Large model had a bed 9 feet long by 46 inches wide. Wheels 40 and 44 inches; track 60 inches. Total weight of wagon was 825 lbs. Note heavy wood hubs used here.

ONE-HORSE FARM WAGON. A more modern vehicle, with iron hubs and riveted reinforcements at outer ends of spokes. A small wagon of this type had a body 90 by 40 inches, with wheels 38 and 44 inches. Weight 500 lbs.; load 800 lbs. Farm wagons along these general lines are still being made by some firms.

COTTON-FRAME AND SEED-BED WAGON. Wheels and gear on this wagon were standard, but body (or bed) was specially designed. Sides of the lower section of the body were 1½ inches thick, plated on top with iron and having "spurs" every 15 inches to keep cotton bales in place. Usual bed was 10½ feet by 3½ feet, with two side sections of 9 and 17 inches in height.

CUT-UNDER WAGON. Both wagons shown on this page were drawn by two or more horses. Note substantial horizontal "fifth wheel" in front center, to give stability and avoid upsetting. Wheels 36 and 52 inches in height.

STUDEBAKER ALUMINUM WAGON. (Period: 1893; scale: half-inch.) For the 1893 Exposition, the Studebaker Company built this lavishly-decorated show wagon. Box made of rosewood, with holly wood border having 35 inlaid medals won by the firm from 1852 to 1893. Three months' labor was needed for woodworking on the body, and thirty processes were used in finishing the rare wood. All metal except tires was of aluminum, fairly rare at that period. Cost: $2,110.

STUDEBAKER FARM WAGON. Thousands of these durable vehicles were built by the firm now famous for its autos. Bodies green with red trim; red wheels.

OIL PIPE GEAR. Formerly used in the oil fields for hauling pipe and casing, this substantial gear could carry up to four tons' load. Shown here in shortened form; the coupling pole was usually 16 feet long. Wheels were 42 and 44 inches, equipped with steel tires (rims) 3 inches wide.

HUCKSTER WAGON. A common one-horse vehicle still used by itinerant vendors, who build their own superstructure to hold boxes, baskets, scales, etc. Body 8½ by 3¼ feet, with sides 10 inches high topped by 7-inch flare boards. Wheels 40 and 44 inches. Drop end-gate. Springs under the seat.

TURPENTINE WAGON. Used in the South for hauling barrels of turpentine. A platform was added to suit, and the wagon was painted with a special mixture which withstood turpentine. Four feet between bolster standards (corner posts) ; wheels 44 and 54 inches. Could haul up to 7500 lbs.

CONTRACTOR'S GEAR. Various platforms and bodies could be adapted to this gear. Built to outwear two ordinary farm wagons. Wheels 3 and 4 feet high.

OX-WAGON. A slightly heavier type of wagon gear, made with either high or low wheels, for use with oxen. Inset above right shows arrangement of end of tongue or pole for attaching ox-yoke. Used with many types of bodies.

KANSAS-NEBRASKA WAGON. Various geographical sections had distinct preferences in wagon styles. This model, used in Kansas, Nebraska, Iowa and the Northwest, had a slightly narrower track. Note arrangement of brake.

FARM WAGON GEAR. This gear had a special type of swivel coupling, shown in detail below. Farm wagons rarely had springs except on seats.

DETAIL VIEW OF COUPLING. This special swivel coupling permitted this type of wagon to move over rough roads and rocky fields with less jolting.

MOUNTAIN WAGON. One of the chief features of the mountain wagon was its oversized brake, shown here. The gear in general was more substantial. Some of these wagons could haul up to 6500 lbs. Body 10½ by 3½ feet; wheels 44 and 52 inches high. Note tool box in front, which also served as foot-rest.

EXTRA-HEAVY WAGON GEAR. Not a city dray, but an extra-heavy gear used on farm and haulage wagons. This gear could carry up to five tons' load. Note brake arm extending upward at rear. Pole shown on ground underneath.

TEXAS WAGON WITH TOP BOWS. Not a "covered wagon" but a 20th-century wagon with bows for a canvas top. Large models weighed 1600 lbs. and could haul three tons. Body 10½ by 3½ feet; sides 28 inches high; wheels 44 and 52 inches high; track 4½ and 5 feet. All woodwork was soaked in oil.

FARM WAGON WITH EXTENSION COUPLER. The "reach" or pole connecting front and rear of this gear had a special coupler allowing hay racks, lumber, etc., up to 20 feet long to be hauled with ease. Note brake arrangement.

TEXAS COTTON-BED WAGON. Used in parts of Texas and Oklahoma. This wagon had an extra-deep cotton bed, with sides 32 inches high. Body 12 by 3½ feet; wheels 44 and 52 inches. All parts were soaked in hot linseed oil before painting, as an aid in withstanding hot, dry climates. Oak hubs.

HAY WAGON. (Period: 1885; scale: five-sixteenths-inch.) This hay wagon, designed in Bucks County, Penn., retained traces of the Conestoga wagon lines. Body was 14½ feet long, 59 inches wide across top, 46 inches wide on bottom. Wheels 46 and 56 inches. Body chrome yellow; gear brown.

MOUNTAIN WAGON. This vehicle, with a body style known as the "California rack bed," weighed up to 1500 lbs. and could haul three times that much. Body 12 feet long, 3½ feet wide, 19 inches high. Wheels 44 and 52 inches high. Equipped with the heavier brake used on all mountain wagons

BEET SUGAR GEAR. Especially designed for hauling large loads of sugar beets from the fields. Could be used with horses, mules, or a train of four or five vehicles could be coupled and drawn by a traction engine. Rear view (top of page) of this massive vehicle shows a "horn" bumper attachment used when the gear was part of a train. Tractor coupling shown on end of tongue in full view below. Special beds with side dumps were used.

FRAME-BED DUMP CART. Used extensively by contractors. Bed was 62 inches long, 40 inches wide, with sides 13 inches high in front and 10 inches high in back. Wheels 54 inches high, with rims two inches wide.

PLANTATION CART. A box-bed dump cart widely used in the South. Body was 58 inches long. Body width: 43 inches in front, 44 inches in back. Sides 13 inches high in front, 10 inches high in back. Wheels 54 inches high. Around 1920, a cart like this sold new for about $55.00.

DUMP CART. Another cart used principally by contractors. The box body, built of 1½-inch hardwood, was hinged to the axles and dumped itself when it was unhooked in front. Body 66 by 44 by 12 inches. Wheels 5 feet high.

POLE TRUCK. For moving heavy materials such as telephone poles and timbers. Frame 42 by 27 inches; wheels 30 inches with a 3-inch tire. The strong axle of this vehicle was of 2-inch round steel. Weight: 340 lbs.

COAL CART. This cart could haul a ton of coal, the load being supported by the axle and not by the horse. Body was 5½ feet long, with 28½-inch sides. Wheels 5 feet in diameter; tire two inches wide. Solid steel axles.

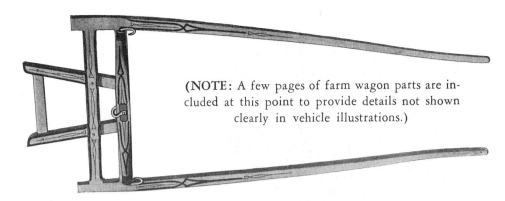

(NOTE: A few pages of farm wagon parts are included at this point to provide details not shown clearly in vehicle illustrations.)

SHAFTS. With this equipment, any drop-tongue two-horse wagon could be converted into a one-horse wagon in a few minutes.

HICKORY AXLE. Axle-bar itself was hickory wood, reinforced beneath by a flat iron "truss." Iron ends, fitting into hubs, were called "skeins."

STEEL ARCHED AXLE. A solid steel bar with an axle cap of black hickory wood "clipped" on. Axles were from 1⅜ to 2½ inches square.

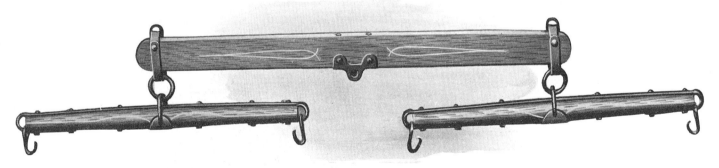

DOUBLETREE AND SINGLETREES. One horse was hitched to each of the two singletrees. Assembly was made of select hickory with iron fittings.

SLIP TONGUE. Left end of this tongue slipped into front of gear. Chains at front were an aid in hitching. This tongue remained projecting stiffly forward and did not drop when the team was unhitched.

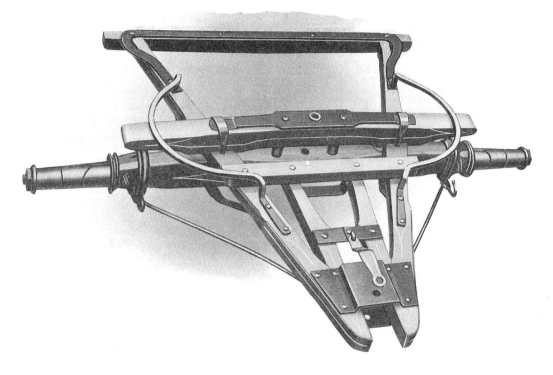

SLIP-STIFF TONGUE FRONT GEAR. Detailed view of front gear assembly
of a modern type, used after 1915. Made of select wood, heavily ironed.

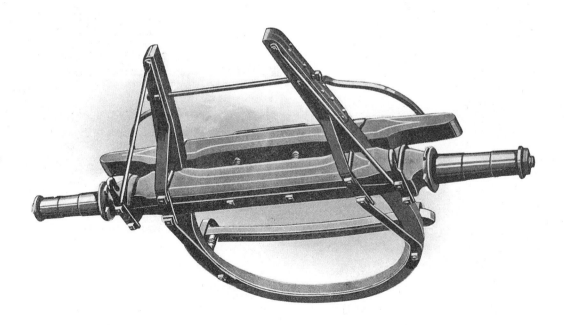

DROP-TONGUE FRONT GEAR. Close-up view from beneath. Drop tongue
with forked rear end fitted this gear. This example shows a high-quality gear.

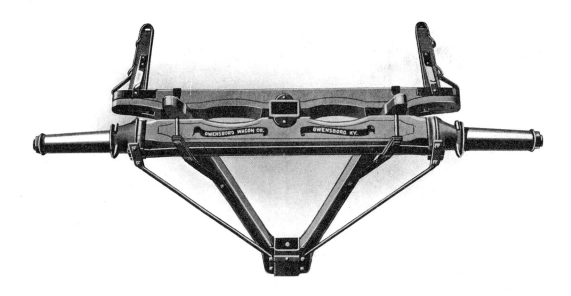

HIND GEAR. Detailed view of rear assembly, viewed from beneath. Since the rear gear did not turn, its design was relatively simple. The "reach" or front-to-rear pole of the wagon passed through the square openings shown. Cross-bar with two posts, above the axle-bar, was called a "bolster."

HUB CONSTRUCTION. View at left shows hub being constructed; view at right shows finished hub. Oak spokes were dipped in hot glue, forced into the hub under tons of pressure, and finished afterwards. View at right shows finished hub partly on the axle skein, inside face of hub at left. The "rim" of a wheel was not a one-piece wooden circle, but consisted of segments, called "felloes," which were joined to make a complete circle.

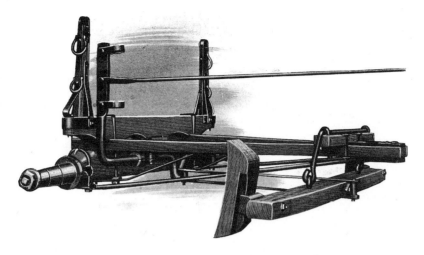

GEAR BRAKE. Detailed view of hind gear showing assembly of a standard type of brake. Upper rod ran forward, and a pull upon it exerted leverage which tightened the brake. There were many different designs of brakes used in different regions, but the basic principles were quite similar.

SEAT. This part of the average farm vehicle was usually the only part offering any riding comfort, but it was a far cry from the riding ease known by modern auto drivers. The seat shows the "lazy back" design.

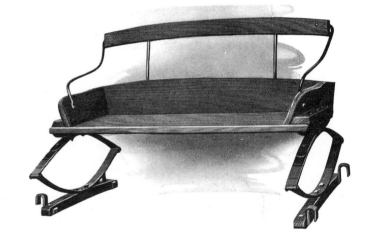

WAGON BED. A perspective view showing construction details of a typical farm wagon box body. Rear end gate was removable, and upper panels of sides and front could also be detached. Pine bottom and sides; oak cleats.

CONESTOGA WAGON. Upper illustration is a modern artist's drawing made from authentic photo at lower right, to convey details more clearly. The Conestoga wagon was first designed in 1755, in the Conestoga Valley of Lancaster County, Pennsylvania. Usually drawn by a six-horse team, its unique construction made it ideal for travel on early trails. It could ford streams, traverse rough terrain without being jarred apart, and had an amazing capacity. Its body design was not unlike that of a seagoing boat. The Conestoga wagon was used in the Alleghenies and west to the Mississippi. Some Conestogas went west, but the true "prairie schooner" of gold rush days was closer to the modern farm wagon in design, although both wagons were used with top covers.

ELLIPTIC HEARSE. (Period: 1865.) This dignified, sombre vehicle, all black, with black upholstery trimmed in silver, and with black plumes, was very deluxe in its day. The body was 42 inches wide; wheels 44 and 50 inches; track 5 feet. Glass side panels; double rear doors with glass.

CIRCULAR HEARSE. (Period: 1870; scale: half-inch.) Note curved glass at front and rear. Body 41 inches wide; seat 30 inches wide. Side glass 76 by 27 inches. Clipped feather plumes. Coffin slid into hearse on a track 18 inches wide with a rail on each side festooned with silver cord. "Hammer cloth" around seat was black and silver. Wheels 43 and 50 inches. All black.

MILK WAGON. In many communities, this "low-down," cut-under milk wagon is still used, in which the driver rides standing. Load capacity was about one ton. Sliding doors. Also formerly used by bakeries. Body 109 by 42 inches, with 6 feet height inside. Wheels 40 and 48 inches.

CHILDREN'S WHITE HEARSE. (Period: 1887; scale: half-inch.) Designed especially for children's funerals, this hearse was built smaller and was finished in white instead of black. Heavy white broadcloth drapes. Body 84 by 42 inches; wheels 36 and 46 inches; 12 and 14 spokes; track 57 inches.

MERCHANT'S WAGON. (Period: 1870; scale: half-inch.) This early delivery wagon had a body with round corners and a rounded top. Painted red, with gold stripes. Body 86 inches long, 44 inches wide, with side panels 12 inches high. Wheels 39 and 51½ inches. Elliptic springs across rear end.

BAKER'S WAGON. A city commercial vehicle hung on elliptic springs. Body 7 feet long, 37 inches wide. Sliding doors and drop windows, all equipped with double-thick glass. Double door on rear end. Wheels 38 and 42 inches.

LUNCH WAGON. These perambulating cafes were drawn to industrial districts by day, and on holidays they were found at fairs or races. At night they roamed wherever business was likely, to serve cabmen and night workers.

OIL WAGON. This battered, workaday example of a tank-wagon indicates how oil was transported in early days. Wagons for hauling or sprinkling water were of similar design. Manufacturers of these special vehicles utilized any suitable, sturdy wagon gear and built the tank to fit the user's specifications.

BUTCHER WAGON. Many housewives, now grandmothers, stood beneath the upraised rear hood of this wagon to inspect proffered meats. Rear view shown above, full view below. These wagons, with bodies 8 feet long, were fitted with steak boxes, cutting block, meat hooks and floor rack. Inside was boarded halfway up and lined with painted duck to the roof. Sliding front.

ICE WAGON. Vanquished by the electric refrigerator and the motor truck was this colorful vehicle beloved by small children. This type of wagon could carry up to two and a half tons of ice. The wagons weighed from 1200 to 2200 lbs. and were equipped with scales, hook, axe rack and box under seat.

PIE WAGON. These wagons made the rounds of early groceries and cafes. Doors slid back; windows could be dropped. Side panels of metal, wood or oilcloth. Body 94 inches long, 37 inches wide, 56 inches high. Wheels 38 and 43 inches. Back had two doors. This wagon could carry a 1300 lb. load.

TIMBER WAGON. Lumbermen bought the front and rear gears and joined them with a "reach" (pole) cut in the forest. Average wagon of this type had wheels 42 and 47 inches high. Such a wagon weighed about 1500 lbs., and some heavier models could haul a six-ton load. Note long brake arm.

PLATFORM-SPRING GROCERY WAGON. (Period: 1885; scale: half-inch.) This wagon was not limited to use by grocers, but was used in many retail trades. The front springs were attached to a "platform" for stability, and such an arrangement was called "platform-spring." Body was 47 inches wide.

THREE-SPRING GROCERY WAGON. (Period: 1884; scale: half-inch.)
Like the example on the previous page, this wagon was not used by grocers
alone. Body shown was 42 inches wide. Wheels 42 and 50 inches, with 14 spokes.
Track 56 inches. Body was green, with straw-colored gear. Silver mountings.

NEW YORK DELIVERY WAGON. (Period: 1884; scale: half-inch.) Built
with strong running-gear to withstand use on hard streets. Glass windows on
sides; one glass in back. Sides curved outward, same curve as back shows.
Body 40 inches wide on floor; wheels 38 and 52 inches. Body green.

BERRY OR FRUIT RACK WAGON. A familiar marketing vehicle, this light wagon had a body 87 by 40 inches, with sides 8 inches high topped by removable racks. Often painted wine color with yellow gear. Wheels were 38 and 42 inches high. Spring arrangement was similar to that of early autos.

WHOLESALE GROCERY WAGON. (Period: 1885; scale: half-inch.) Another vehicle with "platform-springs" in front. White duck, painted cream color, was often used for the sides of such wagons, and the ornamentation is typical. Body was 47 inches wide; wheels 36 and 48 inches; 12 and 14 spokes.

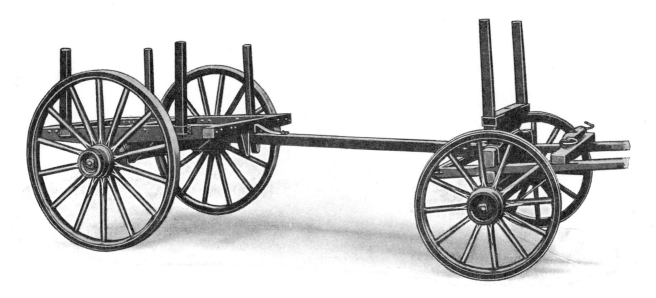

LUMBER BUGGY. The name "buggy" as used here was a lumber-mill term.
Used in lumber yards and woodworking plants, these wagons carried a load
balanced over the rear wheels. Width between uprights was 39 inches. Wheels
40 and 44 inches. Capacity up to three tons. Built of hickory.

DRYGOODS WAGON. (Period: 1885; scale: half-inch.) Commercial vehicles,
drab stepchildren of the early carriage trade, began to be attractive vehicles
in the 1880's. This model, with its "cab front," panelled body, and outswept
sides, was a good example of the trend. Body was 39 inches wide on floor.

DRAG WAGON. This heavy, squat vehicle was used to haul large timbers, beams, etc. One end of the timber rested on the "bolster" of the vehicle and the rear end of the load dragged on the ground. Wheels 30 inches high, with tires 3 inches wide. For use with two or four horses.

LIGHT DELIVERY WAGON: (Period: 1895; scale: half-inch.) Another example of the finer commercial wagon styles which began around 1885. With its neat lamps, cut-under body (painted primrose with navy blue gear) it won an exhibition prize. Body 44½ inches wide; wheels 38 and 50 inches.

LIGHT, OPEN DELIVERY WAGON. A handy vehicle used extensively in towns. Seat equipped with loose cushion. Small model had a body 96 by 40 inches, with 11-inch sides topped by 6-inch flare boards. For one or two horses.

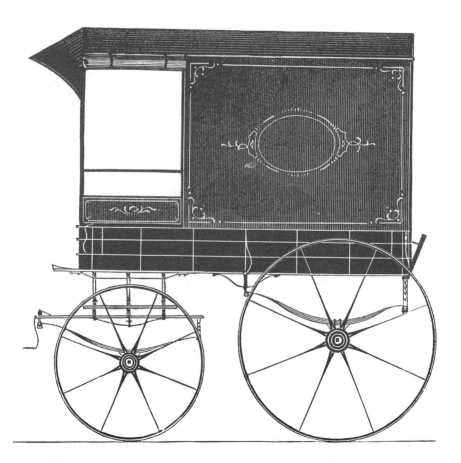

MARKET OR EXPRESS WAGON. (Period: 1870; scale: half-inch.) These rather top-heavy wagons were used in cities after the Civil War. Body was 86 by 45 inches, with lower side panels 12 inches high. Wheels 39 and 51½ inches. Top, which was removable, was 60 inches above the floor. Canvas sides.

FOUR-WHEEL LOG TRUCK. A massive vehicle used by loggers and capable of hauling up to 7½ tons. The horizontal "fifth-wheel" in front kept the gear from rocking while being loaded. Wheels 40 inches high, with 4-inch tires. Wide tires were necessary on softer ground. Drawn by horses or by oxen.

ASYLUM VAN (Period: 1890; scale, half-inch.) Built for use in a New Jersey town, this van was used in conveying inmates of an insane asylum. One barred window on each side; single door in back with a barred window on each side. Lengthwise seats inside. Body 48 inches wide; 22-inch door.

EIGHT-WHEEL LOG TRUCK. One of the most powerful vehicles ever built in America, this truck could carry ten tons of logs. It was drawn by oxen, horses or a traction engine. Wheels 36 inches high, with tires 4 inches wide. Heavily ironed. Fifth-wheel on both front and rear gears.

CITY TEAMING GEAR. Used for heavy hauling in cities, this vehicle could be used as shown to haul pipe, timbers, etc., or could have a platform floor. Wheels 44 and 52 inches high, with 60-inch track. Width between posts was 42 inches. Capacity: up to four tons. Length could be extended.

ARKANSAS LIGHT LOG TRUCK. This type of truck was used only for light logging and had a capacity up to 5000 lbs. All wheels were 40 inches high, with tire 3½ inches wide. Built with a fifth-wheel in front. Heavily ironed.

ICE WAGON. A few of these sturdy vehicles still supply ice in some neighborhoods. Capable of hauling up to two tons of ice, they were drawn by one or two horses. Body of largest size was 120 by 44 inches, with 24-inch sides. Wheels 36 and 46 inches. Scale box was on left side. Slatted floor.

GURNEY CAB: (Period: 1885; scale: half-inch.) Named for its inventor. In contrast to the hansom cab, the Gurney's driver sat in front and passengers entered by a rear door. Four people could ride on the two lengthwise seats. Body was of sheet iron (for sides, roof and floor) on a wood frame. Glass windows. Body 38 inches long, 52 inches wide, 62 inches high. Painted olive green.

HORSE-DRAWN STREET CAR. These cars had a short wheelbase, which enabled them to make the sharp turns required by the tracks. Length of bodies ranged from 8 feet to over 16 feet. There were also summer or excursion cars with open sides and a lighter roof. Some were drawn by two horses.

AMERICAN CAB. (Period: about 1830; scale unknown.) The luxury of springs was generally denied to early American riders in public vehicles. Passengers entered this cab from the rear. Driver rode on top in front.

SEDAN CAB. (Period: 1885; scale: half-inch.) Another cab with driver's seat in front, giving him better control of the horse. Seat was in two hinged sections, lowered after passengers entered from the rear, so they sat facing forward. Body 46 inches wide; wheels 54 inches; track 5 feet. Body blue.

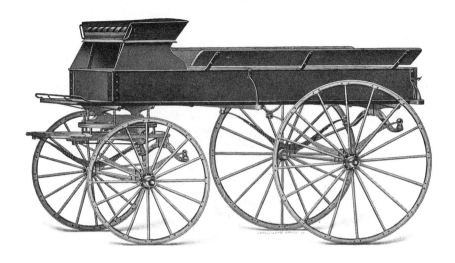

LIGHT DELIVERY WAGON. A relatively easy-riding vehicle for a commercial wagon. Equipped with cushioned seat and three springs at both front and rear. Cut-under front wheels. Fifth-wheel atop front axle. Used by many city firms.

FURNITURE WAGON. A spring wagon especially designed for hauling furniture. Design of the sides permitted ease in lashing loads, and the use of three springs at both front and rear cushioned the load on cobblestone streets.

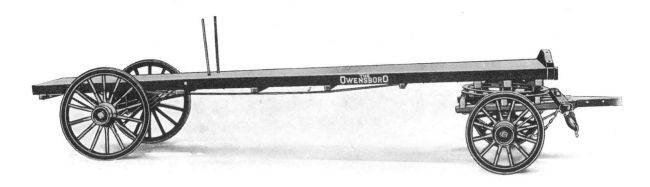

DEAD-AXLE DRAY. This long, heavy dray was often seen bearing immense loads of rolls of newsprint destined for the presses, or it was seen burdened with theatrical scenery. Note heavy hubs and large fifth-wheel in front.

BOTTLE DELIVERY WAGON. (Period: 1890; scale: half-inch.) The designer stated this wagon was "suitable for advertising any type of wet goods." Body was of wood, with neck and cork of bottle made of sheet iron. Shelves in rear of body. Bottle 34 inches square, colored silver. Wheels 54 inches.

DEAD-AXLE DRAY. A lighter type of dray, with no seat or brake, used for loads not requiring a massive dray. Body 126 by 48 inches with sides 12 to 20 inches high. Wheels 34 and 38 inches. For 1 or 2 horses.

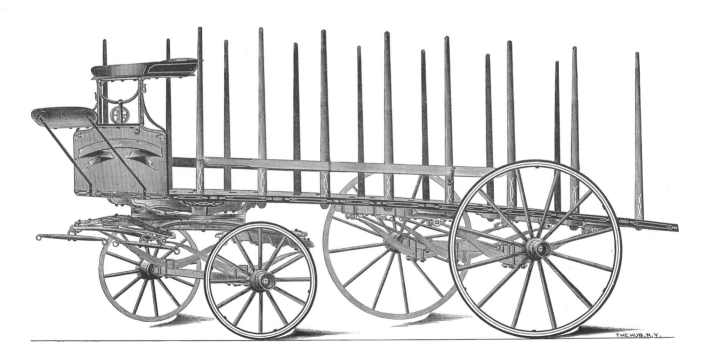

MERCHANDISE TRUCK. (Period: 1885; scale: about three-eighths-inch.) Normandy stallions usually drew these early drays, which were rarely found outside New York City. Some could haul up to seven tons. Body 63 inches wide; wheels 38 and 56 inches high; track 77 inches. Body and gear painted red.

BEER WAGON. This shiny Budweiser wagon, with its spectacular team, has been touring America recently. In bygone days, the beer was hauled in kegs, placed at a slight angle on racks. The beer wagon was a dead-axle dray, with simple racks for kegs. A large canvas parasol was used above the seat.

DRAY WITH STAKE SIDES. This heavy dray had high, chain-linked stakes along its sides and was designed for use with two or more horses. Notice the extra, diagonal braces used on rear axle, typical of drays.

DEAD-AXLE DRAY. Drays could be built to any desired length or width, and it required a capable teamster to handle these heavy vehicles. The example shown had a body 14 feet long and 50 inches wide. Wheels were 34 and 38 inches. Load capacity was up to four tons. Sides 30 inches high.

TRANSFER DRAY. Another long dray used to haul newsprint rolls, theatrical scenery "flat," pipe, poles, and similar loads. Wheels 34 and 46 inches. Bodies were from 9½ to 13 feet long.

LIGHT FOUR-SPRING DRAY. A popular style used for light freight and delivery hauling. Body 108 by 46 inches, with seat not attached and readily movable to any desired position. Box under seat for tools. Wheels 30 and 42 inches. Platform body was plated with iron on top. Could be equipped with brake.

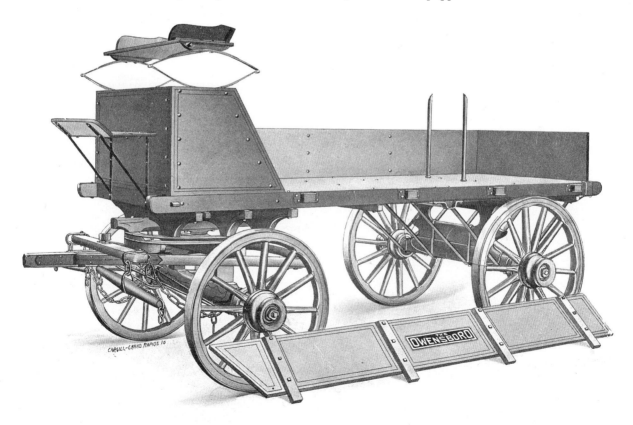

DEAD-AXLE DRAY. As the term indicates, dead axle drays had no springs, which could not be used when extremely heavy loads were hauled. These powerful drays were the mainstay of industry in the days before the truck.

PLATFORM SPRING DRAY. Perched on his seat seven feet above the street, a rugged teamster could manage his team through intricate traffic in the days when such drays thronged city streets. Cut-under front wheels, with chains from axle to doubletree, helped the vehicle turn sharp corners.

FREIGHT AND BAGGAGE WAGON. A heavy spring wagon which approached the size of a dray. Its gear style was known as the "full platform" type. Its dimensions were similar to the four-spring dray shown on page 95.

COAL WAGON. Another heavy vehicle that has lingered on in some sections and which is still seen rarely. Its body was usually lined with iron.

CUT-UNDER COAL WAGON. Similar to the wagon above, but with lower sides. In addition to enabling the driver to make short turns, the cut-under construction also helped a driver to get the wagon out of ruts by turning the front wheels sharply to one side. Note fifth-wheel construction.

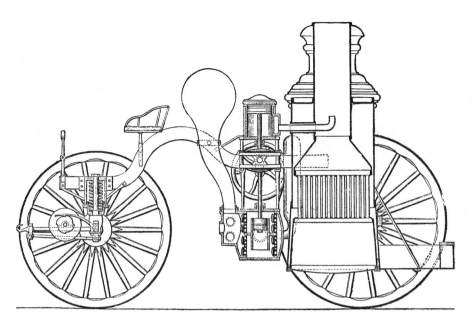

FIRE ENGINE. Generally not considered a "vehicle," the horse-drawn fire engines were still part of the romantic days now vanished. The major types were the Gould, the Button, the Silsby and the Amoskeag. Shown above is a cross-section view of a Gould engine, with a photograph of a Gould-type engine below. (Chicago Museum of Science & Industry photo.)

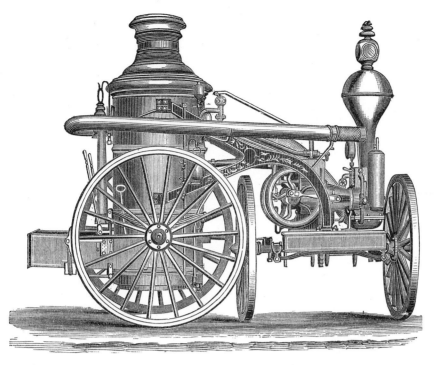

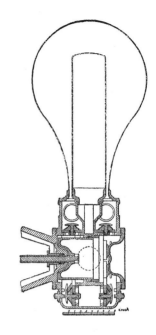

BUTTON FIRE ENGINE. View at right shows a cross section of the pump used on this engine. Button engines were 12½ feet long, 6 feet wide, and 9 feet high. Silsby engine (shown below) was almost identical in size. They weighed up to three tons, could throw a stream 200 feet.

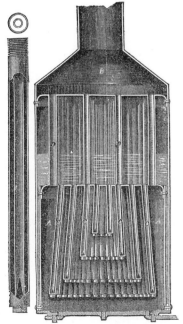

Cross-section view of the boiler of a Silsby fire engine.

SILSBY FIRE ENGINE. In these engines, steam from the boiler entered the engine and moved tooth wheels, which were geared to a pump. A steam pressure of about 80 lbs. was maintained at all times and up to 160 lbs. pressure was used at the fire.

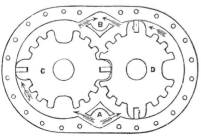

Engine of Silsby steamer.

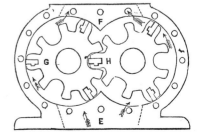

Pump of Silsby steamer.

INDEX TO ILLUSTRATIONS